AMAZING
SCIENCE TRICKS

**Distributed to Schools and Libraries
in the United States by**
ENCYCLOPAEDIA BRITANNICA EDUCATIONAL CORP.
310 S. Michigan Avenue
Chicago, Illinois 60604

Library of Congress Cataloging-in-Publication Data
Charles, Kirk.
Science magic / written by Kirk Charles.
p. cm.
Summary: A collection of magic tricks using science,
including "The Floating Finger Trick,"
"The Dollar Bill Bridge," and "Egg on Edge."
ISBN 0-89565-964-6
1. Scientific recreation–Juvenile literature.
2. Tricks–Juvenile literature. 3. Conjuring–Juvenile literature.
[1. Magic tricks. 2. Scientific recreations.] I. Title.
Q164.C42 1993   92-9012
793.8–dc20   CIP / AC

AMAZING SCIENCE TRICKS

Written by
Kirk Charles

Illustrated by
Viki Woodworth

This Book Is About Magic Tricks Using Science.

It is written by a real magician, whose name is Kirk Charles. Kirk has performed thousands of magic shows, some for school children and some for grown-ups. He has done magic for television shows, commercials and movies. He has also written magic books for magicians.

He wants you to know that he did not invent these tricks. They came from many different sources. Some were learned from books and some were learned from other magicians.

The way to learn the tricks is to do them. So have the necessary items when you read the tricks.

Kirk hopes that you will learn some of these tricks and practice them before you do them. He knows that people of all ages love good magic, and the way to perform good magic is to practice.

If you read something that you don't understand, ask your mom or your dad or your brother or your sister to help. Ask them to keep the secret.

For magic tricks to be wonderful and mysterious, there are certain rules you must follow:

1. Never reveal the secrets of the magic. To do so ruins the magic and spoils the fun.

2. Never tell the audience what you are going to do before you do it. Surprise is very important to making good magic.

3. Never repeat the trick for the same audience during the same show. They will know what's going to happen and will probably figure out the trick.

4. Stories make the magic more mysterious. So make up a story that will go with your trick.

5. Practice each trick many times before you show it to anyone. Without practicing, you might accidentally reveal the secret.

Which line is the longest?
Answer: *They're both the same length.*

The Magicscope

Sometimes we can fool ourselves. This trick does just that.

What happens: By using the magicscope you seem to see through your own hand.

What you need: A cardboard tube of the length that comes with aluminum foil, plastic wrap or wax paper around it.

1. Hold the tube with your right hand and put the tube up to your right eye.

2. Keep both eyes open.

3. Hold your left hand with the palm toward you and place it alongside the tube.

4. Slowly bring your left hand close to your face as you look down the tube. It will look as if there is a hole in your hand. You can see through the hole!

The Floating Finger Trick

Here's a handy trick that can only be seen by the person performing it.

    What happens: A floating finger appears before your eyes.

    What you need: Your own two hands.

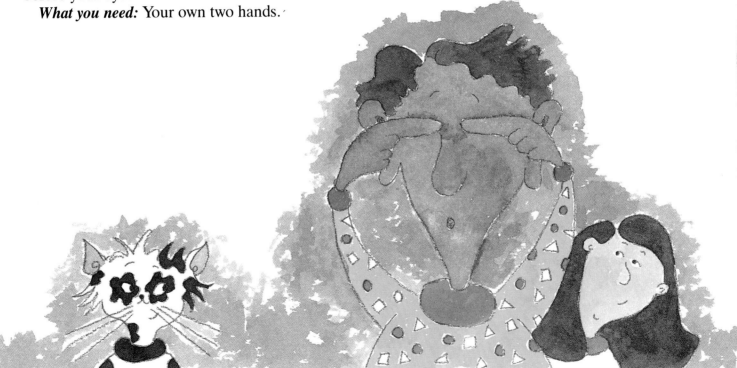

1. Extend the first fingers of both your hands.
2. Touch the very tips of those two fingers together.
3. Bring your fingers up level to your eyes. The fingers should be about three inches away from your nose.

4. Look straight ahead at your fingers.
5. Bring your fingers apart slowly and keep looking at them.
6. With your fingers about a quarter of an inch apart, a third finger will seem to appear between them.

The Upside-Down President

Everybody likes tricks with money. Here's one that you can do.

What happens: You fold the bill with the President right side up. When you unfold the bill the picture of the President is now upside-down.

What you need: A dollar bill.

1. Hold the bill so you can see the President.

2. Now fold the bill in half lengthwise, by bringing the top of the bill down toward yourself.

3. Now fold the left end of the bill toward the right.

4. Again, fold the left end of the bill toward the right. The bill is now folded in quarters.

5. Wave your fingers over the bill and say the magic words, "Alley oop."

6. Now unfold the bill, beginning with the fold the farthest away from you. Unfold it to the left.

7. Now take the next fold to the right.

8. The bill should now be unfolded from right to left, but still folded from top to bottom.

9. Lift the part of the bill closest to you. Bring it up, so the bill is completely unfolded.

10. The President is now upside-down.

The Dollar-Bill Bridge

This trick challenges your friends to do something impossible.

What happens: You ask your friends if they can lay a dollar bill across two glasses, and then place a third glass on top of the bill, so the glass does not fall.

What you need: Three small glasses of equal size and a dollar bill.

1. Place the glasses so they are about three inches apart.

2. Lay the bill across the top of the two glasses.

3. Challenge your friends to put the third glass on top of the bill between the two glasses, so the bill supports the weight of the third glass.

4. Once they give up, offer to show them how it's done.

5. Pleat the bill into many folds. Now place the pleated bill across the two glasses.

6. Carefully balance the third glass on top of the bill. (Sometimes it helps to turn the glass upside down so the mouth of the glass touches the bill.)

The Seven Paper Clips

This is a very old and popular trick. Sometimes it is called "The sheep and wolves."

What happens: Five paper clips seem to change places with two paper clips.

What you need: Seven identical paper clips.

1. Place seven paper clips on the table in this way:

P P P P P

P P

2. Beginning with the right hand, pick up one of the two lower paper clips. The left hand takes the other lower paper clip. There should be a paper clip in each hand. Say, "One paper clip in each hand."

3. With the right hand take the clip farthest to the right. Say aloud, "One."

4. With the left hand take the next clip. Say, "Two."

5. With the right hand take the next one. Say, "Three."

6. With the left hand take the next. Say, "Four."

7. Take the remaining paper clip with the right hand. Say, "Five. We started with one clip in each hand and we added five. Let's count again."

8. Starting with the left hand, put down a paper clip and say, "One."

9. Continue with the right hand, then the left, then the right, then the left. Count as each paper clip is put down. When the fifth one is set down, say, "Five paper clips and one in each hand." (What you really have is two in the right hand and none in the left.)

10. Pick up the clips as before, beginning with the right hand. Make sure you alternate hands. Again, count as you pick each one up.

11. When the last one is picked up, say a magic word and then open your hands to show five paper clips in the right hand and two clips in the left hand.

15

The Magic Glass

In magic, when an object is fixed in some secret way, it is said to be gimmicked. This trick uses a gimmick that you can make.

What happens: A penny disappears and reappears.

What you need: A penny, a large piece of paper, a handkerchief and a gimmicked glass. To gimmick the glass, you will need to glue a piece of paper (which matches the color and texture of the large piece of paper) to the mouth of the glass. Trim the glued piece so it fits the mouth of the glass exactly.

1. Place the large piece of paper on a table.

2. Put the glass mouth down onto the paper. Do these two steps before you show the trick.

3. To show the trick, place the penny on the center of the large piece of paper.

4. Slide the glass across the piece of paper. Put it next to the penny.

5. Cover the glass with the handkerchief.

6. Slide the glass over the penny. Because the small glued piece matches the large piece of paper, it will cover the coin. The coin looks as if it has disappeared.

7. Say a magic word and remove the handkerchief. The coin is gone.

8. Put the handkerchief back onto the glass. Say the magic word and slide the glass back, showing that the coin has returned.

Egg on Edge

Tricks with eggs have been around for hundreds of years. It is believed that Columbus performed this one.

What happens: You balance an egg on one end.

What you need: An egg and some salt.

Before the trick begins, you moisten the bottom end of the egg and put salt on it. The salt will stick to the egg.

1. Show the egg.
2. Place it on the table and carefully balance it.
3. The salt will help cause the egg to stand on end.

No Go Nickel

Here's a puzzle to make your friends think.

What happens: You balance a coin on a card on your finger and remove the card without touching the coin.

What you need: A business card and a nickel.

1. With your left hand palm up, balance a card on your left first finger.

2. Now place the nickel on top of the card. The coin should be balanced on the end of your first finger.

3. Ask your friends if they can remove the card without touching the coin or making it fall.

4. Offer to show them how. Using your right second finger and thumb, snap against the edge of the card. The card will fly out, leaving the nickel on your finger.

The Rubber Pencil

This is an old school trick that has amused kids for many years.

What happens: You make a wood pencil wobble as if it were made of rubber.

What you need: A long pencil.

1. Hold the end of the pencil loosely between the right first finger and thumb.

2. Now move the right hand quickly up and down. This will cause the pencil to wobble.

3. If the pencil does not wobble, you are holding it too tightly between the thumb and finger.

22

Magnetic Balloon

Everybody likes balloons even magicians.

What happens: A balloon sticks to the wall or your hand.

What you need: A balloon inflated with air, also a piece of cloth or fur.

Before the show begins, you rub the balloon against the cloth. Make sure that no one sees you do this.

1. Offer to do an amazing trick with a balloon.

2. Put the balloon against the wall; because of the static electricity the balloon will stick.

3. Remove the balloon and show there is no glue on it.

The Ice Trick

This is a very cool trick.

What happens: You challenge your friends to remove an ice cube from a glass of water using a piece of string.

What you need: A glass of water, an ice cube, a piece of string about twelve inches long and some salt.

1. Show your friends the string and the glass of water with an ice cube floating in it.

2. Ask them if they can remove the cube using the string and without lifting the glass.

3. Offer to show them.

4. Carefully coil some of the string on the top of the ice cube.

5. Pour some salt on top of the string.

6. Wait for about a minute. Then lift the string carefully to see if it's frozen to the cube. If it is, lift the string and the cube will come with it. If the string is not stuck to the cube, wait a little longer or add some more salt.

Long Looks

Here's an optical illusion you can make that will fool your eyes and the eyes of your friends.

What happens: Two colored pieces of cardboard seem to change size.

What you need: Two different-colored curved pieces of cardboard exactly the same size. See the illustration for a pattern you can use. Any two colors will do; for our example we will use pink and green.

1. Place the green arch on the table.
2. Below it, place the pink arch. The pink will look longer.
3. Now move the pink one so it is above the green one. The green one will look longer.

4. The lower arch will always look longer.
5. Then show your friends that they are both the same size.

Knot Impossible

Boy and Girl Scouts are not the only people who can tie fancy knots.

What happens: You tie a knot in a piece of rope without letting go of the ends.

What you need: A piece of rope about twenty-four inches long.

1. Ask your friends if they can tie a knot in the rope without letting go of the ends.

2. Offer to show them how.

3. Place the rope in a straight line on the table in front of you.

4. Cross your arms. The right hand should be touching the upper left arm. The left hand should be touching the upper right arm.

5. Now tuck the left hand under the right arm.

6. In this position, pick up the ends of the rope with each hand. Hold onto the rope.

7. Slowly bring your hands apart. If the rope sticks to your clothing, gently shake it off. A knot will form in the center of the rope.

The Appearing Link

The science of topology gives us our finale.

What happens: A single loop of paper is cut and two linked rings of paper appear.

What you need: A long, narrow strip of paper, some tape and a pair of scissors.

Before the show, cut the long, narrow strip from an old newspaper. Now twist the paper once while forming a loop. Tape the ends together.

1. Show the paper loop.

2. Pierce into the paper with the scissors.

3. Cut down the entire length of the loop.

4. When finished, you will have two linked loops of paper.

December 1995